ALL ABOUT YOU

WAVE

BOOKS

SEATTLE

NEW

YORK

ALL ABOUT YOU

CHRIS NEALON

Published by Wave Books

www.wavepoetry.com

Wave Books titles are distributed to the trade by

Consortium Book Sales and Distribution

Phone: 800-283-3572 / SAN 631-760X

Library of Congress Cataloging-in-Publication Data

Names: Nealon, Christopher S. (Christopher Shaun), 1967– author.

Title: All about you / Chris Nealon.

Other titles: All about you (Compilation)

Description: First edition. | Seattle : Wave Books, 2024.

Identifiers: LCCN 2023041552 | ISBN 9798891060029 (hardcover) |

ISBN 9781950268955 (paperback)

Subjects: LCGFT: Poetry.

Classification: LCC PS3614.E247 A77 2024 | DDC 811/.6—dc23/eng/20230926

LC record available at https://lccn.loc.gov/2023041552

Designed by Crisis

Printed in the United States of America

9 8 7 6 5 4 3 2 1

First Edition

Wave Books 116

Whatever this place is
that we will not admit
to each other we have discovered
is all there is.

—George Stanley

ALL ABOUT YOU

I'M IN

Half already living in the new way
Half attached to disregarded promises

We seem to have gotten lost on the way to the club—

I blame Donal! He and Mike got me into this

Making our way down the middle of an unlit street through a landscape partly
    city partly open plain—

Late-night party sounds from living rooms—empty lots and uncapped
    sewers—it's hard to tell what's occupied and what's abandoned

Adam loops around us on his bike, saying just a couple blocks . . .

Look out! Dead cat—

It's undecayed but plastered to a hump in the grass
Its tail curls pointedly toward an open hole

We peer down into it but Cary tugs my sleeve and murmurs, uhh, live dog?
Pit bull watching from the porch, no leash, no gate—

I startle but he smiles

Later at the bar he says yeah I work in the Tenderloin
I'm always on the lookout for whether things are dead or alive

California seems so far away . . .
Absently he snaps a button on his cowboy shirt

Then he takes a candy wrapper out of his pocket and says, we should use this
Nodding at the darkened door

It's a ticket—gold foil?
I shine my phone light on it—tiny iridescent lines of text flash out

He lets another button go and yep, I'm in

    *

       "This is the work of Memory, when you are about to die
       Go down to the well-built house of Hades. There is a spring on the
          right side, and standing by it a white cypress.
       Do not *even* go near that spring!
       The guards will ask you what you are seeking in the darkness:
       Say, 'I am a child of Earth and starry Sky, I am parched with thirst and
          I am dying; please grant to give me water from the Lake . . .' "

    *

The poem about the body, and the poem above the body
The way you're in one place, and the way you're on a journey

Or maybe I'm just someone who runs errands

Before I traveled to New Orleans I drove back home to western New York State,
      the land of the dead

Watery coffee in the cupholder / Funeral suit in the trunk

Is it a road trip if you're alone?

Chargers and Mustangs, Chargers and Mustangs—

Halfway there and going 85 you're really in the headspace

That guy from Kentucky wants to mess with you but you don't take the bait!
      His license plate reads ALL NUTS

Starting out from Washington was slow

I caught the scent of marshland in a tiny paradise near BWI—but paradise for
      what?

A doe—you see one flash behind the trees—all that muscle built from chomping
      leaves—

And at the marsh's center, nowhere you could step—you'd have to melt or
      somersault into another form—

Traffic picks up and bam! It's Pennsylvania

      *

Back at the bar we've made it to the other side
Yaeji's singing "Raingurl"

The documentarians are draped on couches and snuggling in love seats
They don't seem to hang out with the feature people

There's a lot of pirates in here, and medieval wights, and bons vivants in
       stripper costumes

Wait, how do you dress like a—

PJ and I agree that jumpsuits are hot but why?
Talena: body-length zippers, hello!

The couches are velvet and the walls deep red—

Donal and I start comparing notes on that *Twin Peaks* reboot

I was grossed out by the whole time-loop thing at the end, it just felt like Lynch
       not owning up to his Manichaeism

And haven't we reached peak dead girl
Sorry! Criticism creeping into poetry

What does Vivaldo tell Ida in *Another Country*?
"I'm just a fucked-up group of people"

I'm a two-part person writing out of incompatible moods

It's Planningtorock now
With passerine agility the living and the dead gavotte from room to room

I feel low to the ground but peopled
The disaster has already happened and everyone knows it will come again

I turn to Adam and I ask him, so do you like it here? He grins at me and says, it's
     the best place on Earth

     *

God, church

I grew up in this sanctuary straining to hear a sound
It was Vatican II but Operation Rescue

When my dad couldn't drive anymore my mother would take us to Burger King
     for an hour and make up a homily afterward

But I loved my uncle Art and I'm glad to have something to offer

Brothers and sisters, it begins

       "we know that if our earthly dwelling, a tent,
       should be destroyed,
       we have another building,
       a dwelling not made with hands"

Paul moved around a lot

On Google Maps it looks like it would take you eighteen hours to get from Corinth
     to Ephesus

"This route has tolls / includes a ferry ride / crosses a country border"

Now I feel bad that I edited his letter . . . !
Let me put the God back in

Looking down at the assembled I can see the front door, open
To see the light is almost to walk down the aisle

I could so easily have been that priest after services on some broad lawn in a
    summer breeze, thinking with satisfaction how the Lord made the birches

But I'm on the road back home

    *

It's not the flooding, is it, or the fires
It's not the mass extinction

It's what kind of struggle will this be, and what will we become

What I mean is, will the terminal pressure on the way the rich make us make
    value pit us all against each other?

        Also will we mutate fast enough

The Goldilocks in me is always trying to imagine a remediated future where
    everything is just the right price

The Christian wears me down by always asking me to poke through the material
    world

I've driven myself half crazy thinking I can sift out what's the redemptive part
    and what's the hell

        But not tonight

Outside through the door behind the door a zombie's buying barbecue for
   twenty girls in firefighter costumes

Between two DJ sets you can hear the karaoke down the street

   It's like there's no pure silence

My fears are talking smack about my dreams but I'm not listening

I have been to lots of parties, in expensive capitals and godforsaken little towns

I have found myself at the impossible point where the cyclone meets the
   countercyclone

Have you ever had that feeling where there's just about no difference between
   being ready to dance and ready to go to the wall?

When those chords break through I know that I am not a two-part person, and
   neither are you

You are something unforeseeable—something that sings—

Oh my friends it's going down and we may not survive but liberation beckons in
   all things . . .

ALL ABOUT YOU

What is it—a stream—

If streams were made of grains of pollen—

Almost fragrant—faintly tart—

Your body moving actually and astrally

I never brag in poetry but what are these moments if not the ones in which I know
     what I'm a part of?

A ripple with a brain whose sparks are stars

In memory—a trolley—left on 23rd—

And into the void

       *

OK maybe not the void

That's more a debate than a thing

Emergence, maybe

I do leave fading tracks

Or tracks appear before me as I walk

Shapes of letters, shapes of thoughts—

Are you all at once or in the midst or on your way?

When the valve opens up your body hides behind a tree,

But the valve's behind your body—

You can't tell what tumbles out,

Prisms, dandelions,

Crumpled cloth that needs unbunching . . .

I do like writing

I mean handwriting

I mean writing by hand

    *

Fog—

The needle this morning wavers indifferently

Beauty—not-beauty—

The median and mode of your days—

Impassive sky against your forehead blocking any chance of feeling eager,

But also dulling greed

Something approaches in the lull—

Not exactly beauty but the chance of an answer to your yes-or-no question,

The 8 Ball's icosahedron . . .

Am I even suited to this—

Writing to save your life—pushing on past every clumsy letter—

Hoping for a flower?

"The Magic 8 Ball contains a 20-sided die with 10 positive answers, 5 negative answers, and 5 vague responses"

Shake it, shake it!

That's your sense of form

*

Crashing on a friend's couch like you're 20 again

You wake at dawn—abruptly it's spring—

That thing—connected to the rest of your life—

To life—"rise like a star" is offered you and you don't know why

You flex your hand—so alien—

But pulsing! Why aren't all poems nature poems—

What are poems of deeds—

The temperature rising—the hemisphere begun its tilt again—

Whatever you are—

The groan in your body and the shift in the season—

Like a ward come open—locks allowing boats to pass—

Muladhara—that bum's chakra!—up for anything . . .

    *

This little window with its ledge—my notebook—phone and earbud spilled down
   onto the carpet—playlist queued—crumpled tear-off barcode someone stuck
   to the back of a book from Nightboat—

What's outside? A lot of nearly nothing—February—windows still cracked slightly
   open—rows of rooftop air conditioners—a power plant a radio tower—

Sky—the place the mind goes in its hurry—the wash of cloud is always left to
   right (I'm facing north)—thinned to feather between my "this" and here—

In the book it's 1981—the dawning of the rightward turn—still you smell the
   Hudson in the introduction—

Someone else's river—but you know the feeling—at midlife how you love this
   window—its tiered approach to atmosphere—traversed in a flash by
   starlings—at dusk the flight paths coming into view like math emerging
   from astronomy—

The flesh in the trajectory—the poem inside the phrase—

Nightboat made this book so bracing—it's tangerine and fuchsia and it's not
   apologizing—I watched Doug reading from it at the Project—what was
   audible—a hint of gravel in an older man's voice—it gave the airy upper
   currents of the poems an object to caress—phrases building up to what at

first I thought was crystal pivoting—this way, that way—till a full-on—room warmed up now—let's say whirl—not like avant-garde fast—not pretend-demotic either—just—

Alert—

The bardcode shone—

*

7 now—the air has brightened—

Nico peering out at 6 said look! It's lavender

And it was—though now the haze has taken over,

Mid-Atlantic breezelessness that makes the sky a Heinlein-looking dome of
doom . . .

Really it's just spring

I do always rush to walk the plank,

Sorry, Nico! Superabundance is what I should be teaching you,

Flux and abundance,

Springtime climbing to a view and dispersing into summer,

The violet in the lavender, the time inside the violet,

Abyssal silence and the sound that rises out of it—

It's not just spring . . .

Sweet boy—in the coming days—

What I wish for you—

That stream, glacially cool—

      *

Out of their ocean dreams advance you

I mean they nudge you forward,

Introduce yourself!

Attending a Festschrift that's seated like a banquet,

Celebrating what—it looks like a new Notley epic,

No it's a romance,

In the dream she's Alice—

The page you're asked to read describes the armor Eddie's wearing as he pulls up
     to the chapel,

Black and violet,

Fashioned from an oil spill—

It's beautiful—but hard to read hexameter—

Lucky Anselm! He gets a page composed in the *Alette* stanza

The whole ruined castle has the air of having been repurposed,

Grackles chirring in the high vaults over broken glass—

Some age you never lived in,

Or the wreck of petrocapital—

Your suit fits snugly when you're allegorical,

It's made of woven seaweed . . .

    *

Then your curiosity returns to you

Just a little wet with tears

I welcome it home since I've been wondering—

At evening—what is violet saying—

It speaks to the part of me that wants it both ways

Dim light, square piles,

The prospect of this pen scratching—

And on the other hand, how do we defeat the vampires

I think Kent Monkman gets it

From out of the tempest a wash of color brings the dawn in *Resurgence of the People*

Feather-light and obdurate

The ache could break you but it's also comic

Caliban and Trinculo, sharing a blanket, looking like one animal,

Is that what you wear to the great arrival?

High heels—broken shackles—

    *

Well she said if you put it in a pot you have to water it

Referring I think to poetic form

I am a little proud of these petunias

And though I imagine I prefer the wilderness to gardens I know it's just the wishful
    thinking of the suburbanite

Good morning, weeping cherry

I do still think my favorite kind of line is long,

The flung arm of a dancer,

Maybe dancing for Kyle Abraham,

Trained to let the fingertip release what was launched in the hip,

Saying Godspeed, don't you worry about me—

But lately it's stately,

Like you're hoarding the phonemes in case of disaster—

I stepped away for a second to rummage in the sounds and the sounds became
  an hour

Hey now, says the river birch, I may not sway each day but you don't have to
  tend me

No! I cry—

But it's already happened,

It wasn't even poetry—

Godspeed, you blurt

And off goes your child

  *

"The sky it seems would pour down sinking pitch"

It cracks its knuckles at you, glowering

But you know what Mammatus? Bring it

You can't hide your beauty from me—

I win—

     *

Nightfall

Last scraps in the bird feeder

That one little cloudlet scurrying to find its friends

Vega looks down from on my left and says oh child

Arcturus higher to the right—waving come on, let's run—

Then you let that go

Venus doesn't care about you / you are enmeshed with Venus

I listen to it from a deep recess

It echoes in the quiet where I hear myself pretend to speak in the voices of the
stars

I feel myself aging and I think, an aging man is an aging straight man

I remember feeling being gay meant being close to the edge of unnarratability,

I'd lie in bed and look at my hand and think, are these human fingernails?

Just . . . flesh

I guess you could call that ontological

But come on you guys I'm not gonna become a fucking Heideggerian

The mighty like us thinking, who do you think you are

They stuff us full of scraps of wonder

Chuckling while we Critique the Human

But imagine what a healed people could do

Just flesh—full of chatter—

Hush now

Come on, let's run—

    *

A history of rainy days

Unwritable but in you—

Droplets jeweling a café table on a street you don't remember in a city you
    always will

You cared less back then about your possessions, and more about style

You let the city outfit you

Even now I feel it flex around me

Droplets bead on fabric, ping, dissolve—

Your own cheap clothes perfumed with what you borrowed when you crept out
    of bed,

It filled you once with courage and with curiosity—

Was this the scent they carried into battle? Was this the whiff of victory?

Beauty! Flexing its muscles

Unwritable but liable to find you—even down the years—

What you learned from La Movida

What you learned from Lisa

Style—the next best thing to a breeze

No one says "you can't un-smell that" but think of the rain

    *

Your editor stops by and says, what is this thing with dashes

(I'd promised I'd try commas)

Someone chimes in, but then he'd be writing prose

Someone else says yeah but commas give you contrapposto

Dashes make it all a mug shot

I do approach ideas through my face—

At a rake, though

I always thought I couldn't come in head-on because I was ugly

But it might just be perplexity—

Why this face and not another—

And where do these jolts come from—

You don't have an editor

You have a blinding light

        *

Early mornings by the circle window,

Thumbing through that journal

Your writing is a wash—

I mean a wash of movement,

Ascenders and descenders—

You flip back through seasons of your funny scrawl,

It's spidery and overeager but it has integrity,

A child's sense that maybe 10 degrees is a good tilt for the hand,

That knot of education down in the muscle, carrying the thoughts along,

Or rhythms—is this humming? Woodsmen hum—you play with duration,

Matching it with vowels pealing—

April had a higher ceiling

I mean more assonance than average—a tilt of maybe 10 degrees—

Like your funny angle on America, built on westbound flights with headphones
on—

Relief from paranoia brought by aeriality and melody—

Here comes Gregory—or there he goes—

Keening his outro high above the body of the song,

That end-of-the-novel feeling, no, don't go!

Rue de Départ—

Pam—we're scattered now and long past education—

"Way over yonder in the minor key," remember how you used to hear it as "the
monarchy"?

What a wonderful invention—

And what a beautiful word, yonder

　　*

No way, you think,

I cannot be that field of daisies—

Foolishly you try to run across it,

Fragrance drifting up from underfoot—

Forth and forth as it eludes you,

Sight becoming scent, time space,

The air the sun itself—

You gasp—

Then vertex back into position,

Still a little warmer than the sage was,

The vetiver,

Whose mild infinity you exhale—

High style!

The deep from which all talk begins

Stephanie made you laugh about that

*

Window-washers high above

You forget which tower

A droplet of the profiteering splashes on your jacket and you feel kissed

You always do

Thirsty for life, susceptible,

Accepting it all on their terms—

Shh—ping—like the rain

Bank of America! You have everything I need

And vice versa

Or a droplet of it—

In each exchange the whisper of use

*

Oh shit, you think, and back your way out of the party

Blurting out bad news again

The darkening sky is immense, consoling

You lean against the rail

Freedom, you hum, though you see six hours from now your mind in
    bumper-to-bumper traffic

You live in two worlds

In one to survive is always to be tugging at a cat's cradle built of value—you pull
    on it at somebody's expense, or tilt forward to give them some slack

This involves a constant diet of self-excuse and self-recrimination

It breeds perplexity and fear and a general application of cotton to the ears

In the other world, people know what the hell is going on

It makes you generous and unafraid

Sure, you say, you could keep flogging the singularity but I know you are lonely
out in Menlo Park

You go back to re-direct the course of history, appearing at that café table just in
time to muffle Auden saying "poetry makes noth—"

Phew!

Coming down off time travel is a little bit like coming home from work

Low on electrolytes—you lay down your scythe—

Wasn't that a lily, you think,

As you drift off to sleep . . .

    *

Memory so shy

Approach it head-on and it races away—

Ten minutes later it's peering over your shoulder

Nothing of consequence—a finch, a sparrow

It wants that last farfalle on your plate

And what about you—

A muscle-up, a better clean, a pistol—

Well that's just not what your body's for—

Or not anymore—

How all real change feels like implacability,

Here comes that tropical storm—

Little habits of self-pity and propitiation,

They connect you to some creature long ago who couldn't have conceived of you,

Though it lives inside you—

You hear it in its bitterest mood, saying you were kind to me once,

You taught me language, well at least now I can curse . . .

I wonder if its unmerciful gods are friends with mine

Well—you're on this shore now—storm subsided—

Wanting your mom a little but essentially solid

Or are you—fingers rivulets—

Freer than you thought you were—

You're welcome, says the breeze

    *

Just an early March

Like every seven days a pixel of the kind of fresh perception that kept "Ode to
    Psyche" going

Morning barely blue—only the pines with anything to show

You'll take what you can get

Heroes & models—that feeling of wait, how did you do that, and wanting to read
    it again, again—

Mistaking it for having met them—

I never met John Ashbery

Wait, no, he signed my copy of *Three Poems* in the middle of a blizzard in March
    2009,

I tried to start a conversation—Couperin—

But he just blinked at me with bright blue eyes

Or Schuyler—he sweeps you up in *The Morning of the Poem* on the poem's far
    coast,

You're 50 that day and you wonder if you'll ever write anything so beautiful and
  grumpy

Poor trees—staring blankly—

You've got the wrong spell but they are patient

Late March of 1967—you were just a pixel then—

En route from July,

Fresh from the spray,

From a place you've never been,

July in the pines—

  *

Dark dull break of day,

Food for honesty—

You nod in the direction of all your foolishness, your arrogance, your
    miscalculation

At 15 in Binghamton looking around at the lawyers and thinking, I am outta here

I am going to get a short haircut and listen to 80s music

Day by day your beard gets gray

It links you to your beardless grandpa and the Gulf of Naples,

Trying to make a go of the ferry to Capri—

Flash forward eighty years of American hegemony and you get me,

With my whiskers and a pop sensibility

At 24 in Ithaca quitting after one day of the Gramsci seminar, saying too many
    bros

You didn't exactly choose the wrong side there—

Flash forward thirty years, dudes are rocking out to Carly Rae Jepsen

And haven't you seen an ultra or two get misty listening to "All Too Well"

But dark days are coming

No, they're here—

Sure there's something dickish about saying "I hate the indifferent" but it's not
    like he was wrong, either

At his trial the prosecutor said, "For twenty years we must stop this brain from
    functioning"

Eleven years later his teeth were gone, he was puking up blood

And still we got the *Prison Notebooks*

Of course they got another century for capital, and now their great-grandchildren
    will end up fascist too

But not if I can help it

I have been given too much

At 9 in the craft store discovering pastels and thinking, this stuff is amazing!

Someone should make art with it

At 31 in San Francisco, dropping to your knees in disbelief and gratitude

"I am a partisan, I am alive—"

  *

Dark-bellied clouds—crackling halos—

Proceeding from the south with what you cannot not call dignity

You want to say your animism startles you but it's too quiet for that

Everything in them says come on—their ribboning wake—

You step aside, you step aside,

You almost let your ego go but oh—

Maybe tomorrow

You're getting what you think is smart again and now you've lost the signal—

Wherever myth comes from it's someone's job to keep you from asking

Their boss has need of it—they spring it on you—

You with your forebrain and preferences,

That's the etymology of algorithm,

Or is it—what is it—

Snapped sticks under the decision-tree—

Silk road, stream of pollen,

Dark-bellied whales . . .

*

Midlife: perspicuity! Or crankiness

I have funny sticking points

Like, I don't think the mysteries are best approached in epistemological terms

"More than we could ever know"

Sublimity is a cudgel

Who knows what we can know,

We're still working on it

I don't know why when a friend passes by I slow down anyway

I don't know why I'm such a hugger

I recognize the answer may not be flattering

I hope it has some layers

"Please let there be good in me" is a plea for all of us

I do know why I choose some words

I have ended up at midlife in a complicated argument with literariness

What you know is not technically the winning trick

How far what we know becomes the things we are—there you go

    *

Back in Ithaca—high sky—

Luring you as ever up to Ontario

Vectors, feathers, chevrons—

Something in meridians—

They make you feel like what?

Like your body isn't quite your home

Like, you better go hollow your bones—

Oh, you were always a weirdo

But at least you know the secret meanings

Morning shivers—birds depart in waves—

Goodbye! you cry

And text me when you get there . . .

Whatever demigod October is looks down on you, bemused

Not indifferent—just, it's funny what you think you are

Maybe being just a little bit inhuman makes you a better person?

Out of place in every domicile but loving feeling regional

*

Gray on gray again today—the way you like it—woolly—

You settle in your perch once more and the clouds are like oh, hey, welcome back

At ease with dispersal, like the doves

Four were on a wire just now and now they're gone—moving in accord with their
    magnetic options—

Fields, meridians—

What would that be like

All you have is that tingle at the back of your neck when someone's watching

Though it feels so good when you flex your, uhh, posterior chain—

So deep it's like feeling realized—

And it's true you're motored from behind—

You flex your toes while you put on your contact lenses and feel a little pea-snap
    of pride that you can still be bidirectional

Slyly out of view your monkey brain is saying, bidirectional in time, too, right?

That little spritz of consolation—it disperses like the clouds

*

Autumn again

It clenches its fist

But your open palm undoes the *Ding an sich*

Completely disembodied but very interested in you

The season, that is—

Brown noise on the shag / a ceiling fan / a gust

They each belay? or they support each other

Above you an auroral coloring you haven't seen before,

It must be a reflection from below . . .

Freedom to be nowhere—not rooted—not tragic—

That's what you get from the Susquehanna

You love the poem where the ghosts hunch over the reader's shoulders,

Aching for the material world,

But what if ghosts are breezes—

"Just the arbutus rustling / and the bumping of the logs"

No fame in the waves

No hold no house no beam

Alive as much in temperature as time

END TO END

Something about the way a bicycle can glide you underneath a canopy of trees

Washington unbeautiful to me — but on a warm June night with the camera of
your body on a dolly — golly!

Dusk and relativity

Loft and motion unstick parts of you that had been glued together

The rustle of the mourning doves, settling in above

The raucous laughter coming out of Larry's Lounge

The youthful beauty of the question, are you staying out all night or headed home
to bed?

When you say "you" you're talking to yourself but also to something that can
never respond —

Or which speaks to you in signs and wonders only —

Shallow sleep of summer nights, as though you can't get enough of the sun

Long-missed friends and pop stars peopling your dreams, and interesting
strangers amalgamated from the day

An evening sweat that's mingled with the scent of bay

Some brand—Desert Essence?—in the cavernous bathroom at George and
        Julia's—

Mortality is rich material

The canopy breaks open now and you start to get ahead of yourself

Feeling feeling out in front of you—Standard American English scurrying along
        behind

Composing a poem in your head and hoping that the organizing thought is
        sturdy enough to keep the words in order till you lock your bike and grab a
        pen—

Oh cascade of one-line strophes

They flirt with logic—logic's looking good tonight!—but there's nothing but joy
        to hold them together

You fall like flour through a sifter

Starlight pumping your legs

Ajahn Sucitto says sometimes the citta trembles, have you felt that?

Tissue paper in us—is us!—we're made of layers

Adorno says philosophy in Hegel rustles and murmurs,

Which always makes me think of ball gowns—but axially these trees—

Creaking—sighing—

I think the people in charge of the "continuous nerve movie" are Italian
     Neorealists

(I like to think that Philip Whalen would laugh at that)

(And yes this is a scene of life at the capital)

Lightning lighting for an instant the forked path of the neurons,

What will you choose?

I choose phyllo dough and phylogenesis

Something animal in us—appropriated for the purpose of building a society

Early mornings—people yawning—testing out from under bedsheets their
     suitedness to teeming life

And time teems—19th, 18th, 17th Streets, lined with trees—disclosing evening
     gloaming—inside one June night a whole September—

Light of lights—kind because receding,

What does it have to lose? It makes space for you

I love reductions in glare, you can see the taupe of the doves

Brick looks handled

Things are clear as miniatures, with a whisper of air between them

Dents and buckles in the earth

You walk your portion of it with a socially average amount of swagger

Feeling a joy in strength that doesn't need an arrow or a sword

Just this humanness, alert, bipedal

It has no narrative or climax but it shines out as substance

3rd Street upon you—

Hop off, hoist the frame, lock it to the rail

Still so much activity in the freshly drawn-down dark, it glitters somehow

How do these bees know where to go?

What is it that bursts from gems?

Some late light that you mistake for nothing

You didn't speak a word the whole ride long

And no one would have noticed you, flitting past, leaving little gaps in the present,

Beelike making substance of them,

Though you can't know that, can you—you were wandering the world,

Just as you'll forget it ever happened,

Reaching for your keys,

Streetlight filtered through the gate of myrtle . . .

HI, JULY

Last sweet night of the three-day weekend

You lean your bike against the barbed-wire fence and press your face into the
mesh

Down long lawns and to the Capitol below (three miles away) your eye realizes
there are still fireworks—at least on the Virginia side

A breeze rushes up to meet you and you exhale in reply

A part of you thinks, you are very theatrical with your headphones on and your
back to the sidewalk

The H2 rumbles by on Michigan Avenue, ambulances race to their bays, and
the H2 again, and joggers, and kids on scooters

A police helicopter sweeps overhead

And fireflies, of course, on the great treeless lawn

The grip of your hands on the web of wire makes you feel alive

You think of friends from long ago—friends far away

I'm sorry, you think, and thank you—

The breeze becomes a night wind—joy itself—ceaseless, improbable

Remember that trip?

Oh no, a voice inside you said, you are way too philosophical for these
mushrooms

Greedy for knowledge instead of riding the wave

But I did feel free when it entered me

There was a dark period where I was doing yard work?

But the lecture sounded extra good

I could hear Mike laughing when I thought, I like my dharma teachers SO MUCH

I hear so many voices in my head, is it all voices?

It is not

There's a kind of high noon to these things, isn't there, face of god, abyss of
time,

But when at dusk you return to people you can see that in the flowering of their
particularity they are not the lowest rung

Disturbingly there are no rungs

Loving them is grounding though—speciation's grounding—and it's also just
that, love

The sadness under the sadness

The gall beneath the bile

One black, one blue

And underneath them both a nectar, hiding in the empty dark around the word
"you"

The word that taught you how to be a person

In a rapture in the back of the car, 8 or 9 years old, singing softly but with all
your heart to "Haven't Got Time for the Pain"

Launching a life of referring to singers by their first names, so gay!

It's hard to be a person—holding all your demons at bay

Grasping after substance that eludes you because it eludes itself

At some point you had to say, hey now, exhale, matter doesn't hate you, it's just
. . . busy

I'll tell you who hates you

Both the hill I'm standing on and the object of my attention have been removed
from the maps

Up until January you could type in "National Capitol" and figure out how long
it would take you to bike up to the reservoir, or get a sense of the gradient

Well I don't mind—let them have it

Somewhere a difference in temperatures has produced this wind, which won't
    stop caressing your body

Katell is singing, "well I am bold now babe . . ."

Heart-pounding glories I couldn't share with you, we were too harried, you
    were too young—

But there are times when time is like a three-day weekend

You find a way to leap for a second up the slope—to say, my face was a mask of
    worry but I loved you even so—

Hot tears / bad blood / beautiful day

Who will stand here in a hundred years?

What memorials will you attend?

You didn't notice that when you were young,

The way the earth exhales to let someone in—

It all falls apart, matter thinks, but that was an amazing party hat . . .

Your bike light blinks against the fence,

And the cup passes to you.

AWAKEN'D EYES

The bored god visits you and you sit bolt upright

It probes your brain

It's weird to feel so . . . sifted through

But I guess he found the password

Look up, she says

The pattern of the shadows on the house across the street impossibly complex

And the budding midsize tree in front of it, under streetlight—a tree and a prism

To be accompanied—the feeling brings a kind of rhododendron up in you

It has a reach in all directions—it makes a net around your nakedness

Dance for me, the god says

Uhh, OK

The 90s, the bay

That feeling of a sprawling geologic gift

Even all the oil tanks heaped on Richmond couldn't kill it

Sitting on porches in the Berkeley hills at dusk and watching lights come on
across the water like the houses on the other side were embers in a hearth

Or we were one, and San Francisco was watching us flicker

The mesh of streets that made the Mistro

Jasmine in the planters on the sidewalk—bougainvillea trellised on front gates

Back when giant ginger Joel was manager at Jumpin' Java, really the DJ

The day he sent a lightning bolt through us—the boy to my left going what is
that (my ears pricked up) and the too-cool one next to him like, they're
called *Deaf Punk*

I remember all the flowers but I can't recall the birds

I do know that you can call the mourning doves back East (I'm here now) by a
whole little range of alternate names

Charles Lucien Bonaparte officially designated them Zenaida doves, in honor of
his young wife

Who was also his cousin

"When she was 14, Napoleon offered Zénaïde in marriage to Ferdinand, the
deposed king of Spain, but the offer was refused"

She spent a brief period of exile in . . . New Jersey

Princess of Canino and Musignano, whose name means "life of Zeus"

Zénaïde! I too have felt the distance between the god in me and my workaday
    existence

Heavily encased in an MRI—neck brace, ear plugs, a blanket, a shunt

Tears running down my cheeks from the sweet acoustic music they let me choose

I can hardly hear anything—it's just that the music exists

Look up, says the technician, and sure enough there's a strip of mirror above my
    head

You're done, she says, and you're back on the sidewalk—floating above yourself,

Like reading something you wrote—

A year ago I wrote, Oh sweet Rob (he broke both arms)—

Who was I writing to, did I think I'd forget?

Sweet to imagine—old man me squinting over my scrawl and going oh, I
    remember now . . .

"What will become of us" is a sentence I've been spared but I have felt that chill

A maw—Ananke—

You want to say it's inky but the night is starry—

What my dad stepped into—the downward spiral of his last few breaths—

The flash of his eyes above a sudden final smile

Scent of disinfectant, sun too strong in the room—

Fate wore particulars

Looking back at us arrayed around that bed we were what, tableaued?

"All phenomena" is more like it

So what is this exhilaration, if you're just a thing

When the geese fly by—how does that feel so real—

And what does that make of the knot in your heart?

Were you afraid of being born?

Did you think, if I'm a wave, how will I find them?

When I look them up Canino and Musignano are described as "two neighbouring
    villages"

At the end all that's left of you is a kind of dry stick with a smile painted on

But the smile is real

"I believe in love" is a deep sentence

Expect to find it on your deathbed, says the god, if you die in a bed

WAIT A MINUTE

Clear pink sky at 7 a.m. — or mostly clear —

You can't rush spring but your body has big plans

Hey now, get back in here!

All your senses mobbing their gates like children pressing against a fence

Thin high clouds indifferent and alluring

Just the other morning they were thick and definitional — and that got you all
     excited, too

The sky — its rhetoric — it reaches and reaches and becomes poetics

To call Ontario "blue," just the right way — it does more than state the obvious —

It gives you a channel for your excitement,

Is that what patience is?

The C&O Canal —

Me and Rob and Nico and heading down to see if we can get a glimpse of the
     painted bunting improbably wintering in Maryland

That was fun—to seek, to find—climbing boulders, chatting with birders,
    getting the gossip—

All of us arrayed below the road, at the bottom of a steep grade, when he finally
    appeared, shining out tropically from under dormant vines,

A ripple running through us all—

A bald eagle coasted low over the road above us—I mean really low—and
    everyone was like whatever

What is it about awaiting arrivals—alert at the gate with your tail wagging

Or setting the picnic table on a warm June day with Hölderlin, hoping the
    Olympian gods will show up

When they finally do it's September and they're Valkyries

Imagine the pulse sounding out like a terrible announcement at the beginning
    of the Modeselektor remix of "The Dull Flame of Desire,"

Actually just listen to the whole thing, I can wait

Everything in that sound says leave the car running, we are not fucking around

Which makes it all the more astonishing that when their spaceship lands they
    speak to you in the language of Sappho 16

I mean they coo to each other: I love this about you, dear, also this—but *this*—

Now that's love

Metallized but porous, running fingertips over the mortal world, exhaling on the
    cheeks and foreheads of the slain

When they leave you slump exhausted in your seat, feeling vaguely swanlike and
    ungendered

Something about that extra minute or two—the club version instead of the radio
    edit—you start to notice clouds in motion,

They have big plans—this bank of feathered cirrus—it's like they voted to say
    forget the Coriolis effect, let's move west to east

The DJ playing "Precious Box" at the Powerhouse, a song about crushing
    loneliness and captivity to mass media with lyrics so wending they feel
    Jamesian—

Moving entirely opposite the energy of the men in those rooms

The Powerhouse was naughty

Or that moment when you realize that the club's been throbbing to a song about
    the Fates

"So tell me how do you do? / Finally I meet you . . ."

Well you have your playlist now, what should we call it?

That part of us that feels connected, to life, to world—it's slower to rouse—
    has further to travel—and it always steps aside for bossy dopamine—

Like some deep-sea turtle that could save us all

Oh! To be unruled by fight-or-flight—to get behind political dread and this
    terrible what is it catalepsy—

It seems like the project of a million lifetimes,

At least until you live them all at once

Why is it so humanizing to be able to wait,

And why are epithets so beautiful?

"Patience—the incinerator—

of all the torment in the heart . . ."

STEMS IN A JAR

And what about ugliness, you?

Who staked it all on beauty

That was a mistake . . .

Humid August predawns—you hunch beside the fan

Wet paper towels on the sidewalk,

That mulberry tree I've hated for so long . . .

Choking out the hollies and the chinaberry

Look at me! Critiquing the shapes of soggy leaves

Colleen and I used to call it "the muck"—kind of meaning the East Coast—

Then David would chasten us with a lecture on fantastic fungi

Intellectually I'd be convinced but it would never quite stick

January—Seneca Creek—the wetlands are cool in a science-class kind of way but
that grove of pines behind the parking lot . . . you sense it on the wind and
think, now *that's* nature

Why does your whole body rush there?

All I've come up with is, past life—a million of them

Spore-star, tree bark, half-man, half-beast

Sighing on its bed of needles

It's so perfect it's hard to like anything else,

Or so you think,

The forest tuning and re-tuning itself until even the churn of the muck seems
   lovable,

Though its message is your own dissolution—

At least it's not a hymn to war

Fratboy shenanigans in the eclogues—

Silenus wakes roped to a mulberry, face smeared with juice,

The shepherds snicker, leer, demand a song—

Well—

Demigod hangovers don't last long

My dudes, he goes, no need for bondage, give me a sec

He clears his throat

Then depending on which translation you read you'll get a different melody

"For Silenus sang first of atoms . . .

Gathered dancing across the deep . . ."

Or:

"He isn't a surgeon, a dentist, or an engineer.

All he does is make the sun come up . . ."

All creation shaking to the rafters

Alleluias born of something ugly

Morus alba—I think it means "Stupid White Tree"?

Morus / moron / "foolish, silly, pixilated,"

Pixilated?

1. behaving in an eccentric manner, as though led by pixies
2. whimsical
3. drunk

Mulberry—bark of laughter—

With the prospect upon us of universal war I find my thoughts have turned
    more kindly to all the Mushrooms at the End of the World

Opening and opening your heart

Virgil's attention in that poem never returns to the shepherds, it just keeps
    moving outward, Venus glittering at dusk,

Creation song become a song of legends

I always blink and miss that

Like how does limning what we're made of become the tale of what we do?

And if matter is an accident, will we ever get out of this mess?

I think it's Simone Weil who says it's not about the action in the *Iliad*, it's about
    the light the action happens in,

Light of pity and compassion—

I may be getting that wrong

But I have seen us in it—

Dinged along the way,

Pockmarked,

A sentence buried in our bodies with an asterisk that glitters in the brain

Eclogue—analogue—

The ding of a spoon, the gong of a deed,

The beautiful lofty things we do that we can't see—

Making gestures for each other out of the churn,

Blinking at the blades of the fan,

Asking will I ever be able to know what paradise is,

Saying that will happen, but you won't understand.

ACKNOWLEDGMENTS

The epigraph to this book is taken from George Stanley's poem "Paradise Shelter," in *A Tall, Serious Girl: Selected Poems: 1957–2000* (Qua Books, 2003).

"I'm In" includes a lightly adapted version of Fritz Graf and Sarah Iles Johnston's translation of the Hipponion lamella in Michele Asuni's translation of Maria Michela Sassi's *The Beginnings of Philosophy in Greece* (Princeton University Press, 2018). "Wait a Minute" contains lines from a talk by Gil Fronsdal. "Stems in a Jar" contains lines from translations of Virgil to be found in Nate Klug's *Rude Woods* (The Song Cave, 2013) and David R. Slavitt's *Eclogues and Georgics of Virgil* (Johns Hopkins University Press, 1990).

I would like to thank the editors of the following magazines, in which versions or parts of some of these poems appeared:

> *Boston Review*: "I'm In" (published as "All In")
> *Harper's* and *Ariadne Magazine*: sections of "All About You" (published as "The Book of Breezes" and "La Central")

"I'm In" is for Kevin Killian.